Broadman & Holman Publishers
Nashville, Tennessee
First published in 1998 by ADC International, Belgium
This edition published under arrangement with
Ottenheimer Publishers, Inc., Owings Mills, Maryland
© 1998 A.M. Lefèvre, M. Loiseaux, M. Nathan-Deiller, A. Van Gool
Editorial Director: CND/Muriel Nathan-Deiller
ISBN 08054-9342-5
All rights reserved. Printed in Dubai
BI083A

THE GREATEST STORIES
OF THE NEW TESTAMENT
STORIES of JESUS

BROADMAN
&HOLMAN
PUBLISHERS

MARY IS VISITED BY AN ANGEL

During King Herod's reign, a young woman lived in Galilee, in the town of Nazareth. Her name was Mary, and she was betrothed to a young carpenter called Joseph. One morning an angel appeared to Mary. "Do not be afraid, Mary," he said. "The Lord has sent me with a message for you. He has chosen to honor you above all women. Soon you will bear a son, whom you will name Jesus. He will be called the Son of the Most High, and his kingdom will last forever."

"How can this be," asked Mary in wonder, "since I am a virgin?" And the angel told her, "The power of the Holy Spirit shall come upon you, and you shall bear the Son of God."

Mary bowed her head. "I am the servant of the Lord," she replied. "It shall be as you have said."

*(**Luke 1**:26–38)*

THE BIRTH OF JESUS

The Israelites who had settled in Judea and Galilee were now known as the Jews, and Herod was their king. But the most powerful ruler in all the land was Augustus, the Roman emperor.

Some months after Joseph and Mary were married, Augustus wanted to know how many of his subjects lived in each country. He gave the order that all persons must return to the town of their birth, to sign a register. Joseph and Mary traveled to Bethlehem, where Joseph had been born.

But when they arrived, the inns were full, and they had to stay in a stable. Here, Jesus was born.

That night an angel appeared to a group of shepherds watching their flocks in the fields. "I bring you joyful news. Christ the Lord has been born to save mankind. You will find him in a stable, lying in a manger. Go now to Bethlehem and honor him."

*(**Luke 2**:1–20)*

THE VISIT OF THE WISE MEN

Far away in the East, wise men had seen a new star in the heavens. They followed the star to Jerusalem and came before King Herod. "We seek the child who has been born King of the Jews," they told Herod. "We have come to worship him." It had been foretold that the King of the Jews would be born in Bethlehem. Herod asked the wise men to send word when they had found the child. "For I wish to honor him myself," he said.

When the wise men found Jesus, they bowed before him and worshiped him. They had brought him precious gifts of gold, frankincense, and myrrh.

That night an angel came in a dream and warned the wise men not to return to King Herod. So they went back to their country without traveling through Jerusalem.

(Matthew 2:1–12)

Herod had lied to the wise men, for he did not want to worship Jesus at all. He wanted to kill him. "The Jews will make him their king, and he will be more powerful than I!" he said.

When he realized that the wise men were not going to return, Herod was furious. He ordered his soldiers to go to Bethlehem and kill every boy child under two years of age. But the angel of the Lord appeared to Joseph in a dream and warned him: "Your child is in danger. You must take shelter in Egypt." Joseph took his family and left Bethlehem that same night, and they made the long journey into Egypt.

After some years in exile they learned that Herod was dead, and they returned to Nazareth.

*(**Matthew 2**:13–22)*

JESUS IN THE TEMPLE

Every year, Joseph and Mary went to Jerusalem to celebrate the feast of the Passover. When the festival finished, they would travel home with a large group of friends and family.

One year, when Jesus was twelve years old, his parents suddenly realized that he was not with them. Joseph and Mary hurried back to Jerusalem. Frightened for his safety, they searched for three days. Finally they found him in the temple, where he was talking with the priests and teachers. He amazed everyone with his knowledge and wisdom.

"We were so worried about you, my son," cried Mary. But Jesus replied simply, "You need not have searched for me. Where else would I be but in my Father's house?"

(Luke 2:41–52)

THE BAPTISM OF JESUS

Mary's relative, Elizabeth, also had a son. His name was John and he lived as a hermit on the banks of the Jordan River. People came from all over Judea to hear him preach and to beg forgiveness for their sins. After they had repented, he baptized them in the river; so he became known as John the Baptist.

John told his followers about the prophet Isaiah, who many years before had foretold that a savior would be sent to them. Some people thought that John was the savior. But he told them, "I baptize you with water, but one greater than I will baptize you with the Holy Spirit."

When Jesus was a young man, he went to John, who baptized him in the river. As Jesus stepped out of the water, the Holy Spirit came down upon him. The mighty voice of God spoke from heaven, "This is my Son, whom I love."

(Matthew 3:1–17; Mark 1:1–11; Luke 1:57–66; John 1:19–34)

16

THE TWELVE APOSTLES

Jesus traveled into Galilee to spread the Word of God. In every town he visited, crowds gathered to hear him preach. "The kingdom of God is near," he told them. "It is time to repent of your sins." One day, Jesus passed two fishermen casting their nets into the sea. They were Simon and his brother Andrew. "Leave your nets and follow me," Jesus told them. "I will make you fishers of men."

Simon and Andrew did as Jesus asked and became his first disciples. More disciples joined him as he traveled, and one day Jesus gathered them around him. From them he picked twelve to be his Apostles.

These twelve were Simon (known as Peter), his brother Andrew, James son of Zebedee, his brother John, Philip, Bartholomew, Matthew, Thomas, James, Thaddeus, Simon, and Judas Iscariot.

(Matthew 4:17–22; 10:1–4; Mark 1:14–20; 3:13–19; Luke 5:1–11; 6:12–16; 9:1)

THE WEDDING AT CANA

In the town of Cana, Jesus was invited to a wedding. The Apostles were with him, and so was Mary, his mother.

After some time, Mary saw that the wine had run out. She told Jesus, and Jesus told the servants to fill six large jars with water. "Now fill a cup and take it to the host." The servants did as he told them.

When the host drank from the cup, he turned to the bridegroom. "This wine is superb. Most people serve the best wine first and save the cheaper wine until the guests have drunk too much. But you have served your best wine last."

Then Mary, the servants, and the Apostles realized that Jesus had turned the water to wine. This was the first miracle that Jesus performed.

(John 2:1–11)

21

THE SERMON ON THE MOUNT

Word of Jesus spread throughout the land, and wherever he went, large crowds gathered to hear him. He healed the sick and brought comfort to the poor and needy.

He preached to them of the kingdom of God and how they could attain it. "Those who are sick or poor or hungry should rejoice, for they will receive their reward in heaven. But those who are rich and seek material gain on earth will find no comfort there."

He preached compassion, humility, and obedience to the commandments. Those who heard him were amazed by his words, for no one had ever spoken like him before.

(Matthew 5:7; Luke 6:17–49)

$\mathscr{T}$HE PARABLE OF THE PRODIGAL SON

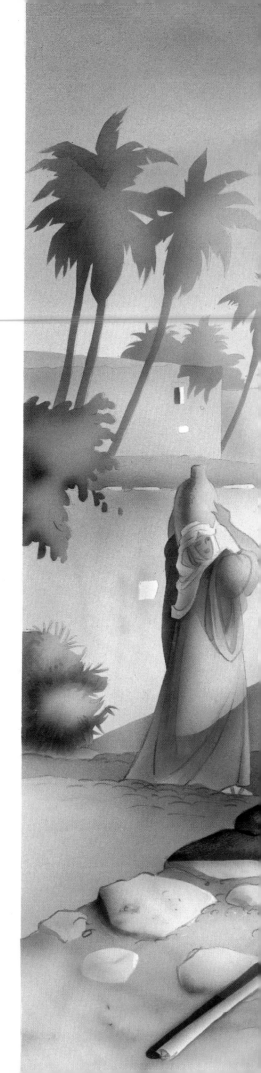

Jesus often preached in parables, so that those who came to listen would more easily understand the Word of God. One day the lawyers were mocking him for welcoming the company of sinners. "One repentant sinner brings more rejoicing in heaven than ninety-nine good men who do not need forgiveness," Jesus told them.

"Once there was a man with two sons," he continued. "The younger asked for his share of money, then spent it recklessly. When he had none left, he decided to return to his father and beg forgiveness for his behavior. Humbly he went home and asked his father to treat him as a hired worker, for he was no longer to be called his son. But his father called for a great feast to celebrate his son's return. The elder son was angry because he had worked hard for his father but had never received such splendid treatment. 'My son,' explained the old man, 'we must celebrate because your brother was lost to us, and now he is found.'"

*(**Luke 15**:1–32)*

THE WORKERS IN THE VINEYARD

Jesus explained to his followers that those who trust in earthly possessions will not reap rewards in heaven. Then he told a parable that shows God gives according to grace, not merit.

"A landowner hired men to work in his vineyards and promised to pay them one coin," he told his listeners. "Toward the end of the day he saw men who still had no work and sent them to his vineyard too. When the work was finished, he paid his workers, beginning with those who had started last. He gave each of them one coin. Those who had worked since the beginning of the day expected more money. When he gave them one coin also, they grumbled that they had done more work than the others. The landowner explained that he would treat them all the same."

Jesus explained that no one gets less than he was promised. And all get more than they deserve.

*(**Matthew 19**:23–30; **20**:1–16)*

THE PARABLE OF THE SOWER

When a large crowd had gathered, Jesus said to them, "A farmer went out to sow his seed. As he scattered it, some fell on the path and was eaten by birds. Some fell on rock, and the plants withered on the dry ground. Some seed fell among weeds that choked the plants. But some seed fell on good soil, and the plants grew strong and plentiful."

When the disciples asked Jesus what the parable meant, he explained to them: "The seed that falls on the path is like those who hear the Word of God but do not believe. The seed that falls on stony ground is like those who hear but do not maintain their faith. The seed choked by weeds represents people who get distracted by earthly worries.

"But the seed that falls on good soil stands for those who show their true conversion by maintaining their faith and producing the fruit of obedience."

*(**Matthew 13**:4–9; **Luke 8**:1–15)*

31

JESUS HEALS THE SICK

One day some men brought their crippled friend to see Jesus. This friend was paralyzed, and they carried him on a mat. There was such a crowd around Jesus that the men climbed up onto the roof and lowered their friend into the room below.

When Jesus saw how strong their faith was, he healed the crippled man. "Friend, your sins are forgiven," he said. "Take your mat and go home."

Another time a Roman soldier approached Jesus as he was entering a town. He told Jesus that his faithful servant was dying. "I will come to him," said Jesus. But the soldier replied, "I do not ask you to go to my home, for I am not worthy. But only say the word and my servant shall be healed."

"Never have I seen such faith as yours," said Jesus gladly. "Your servant shall live."

(Matthew 9:1–8; Luke 5:17–26; Matthew 8:5–13)

JESUS WALKS ON THE WATER

One day Jesus was teaching in a very remote place. As it grew dark, the Apostles told Jesus that he should send the people away. "They will be hungry soon, and we have nothing for them here."

But Jesus took five loaves and two small fish and divided them among the Apostles. "Pass this food around the crowd." The Apostles did not know what to think, for there were many people in the crowd. But they did as Jesus asked. To their amazement, there was plenty of food for everyone.

After this miracle, Jesus went to pray by himself. The Apostles took a boat to the other side of the lake, but a strong wind blew up, and they became worried.

Suddenly they saw Jesus walking toward them across the water. They were terrified, but Jesus called out to reassure them. "Come to me, Peter," he said. As soon as Peter stepped from the boat, he became afraid. "Help me, Lord!" he cried. "I will sink." Jesus helped Peter back on board. Jesus asked him, "Peter, why did you doubt?"

*(**Matthew 14**:13–31; **Mark 8**:1–9; **Luke 9**:10-17; **John 6**:1–21)*

35

THE TRANSFIGURATION

Jesus took three of his Apostles, Peter, James, and John, to the top of a high mountain. There Jesus was transfigured. His face shone as brilliantly as the sun, and his clothes became a blinding white. The prophets, Moses and Elijah, appeared beside him, bathed in the same light.

A bright cloud came down around them, and the Apostles heard the voice of God. "This is my beloved Son. Listen to him."

In terror the three Apostles fell to their knees. Jesus reached out to them and told them not to be afraid. "You must go back now. But do not speak of what you have seen here until the Son of man has risen again."

The Apostles left Jesus, puzzled by his last words.

(Matthew 17:1–9; Mark 9:2–13; Luke 9:28–36)

JESUS AND THE CHILDREN

Wherever Jesus went, parents brought their babies for him to touch and bless. Little children gathered around him as he preached, all trying to get as close to him as they could.

The apostles thought that the children were bothering Jesus by crowding him. They tried to chase the children away, but Jesus stopped them. "Let the little children come to me. You know that the kingdom of God welcomes the weak and the small. You have heard me say this many times."

He pointed to the smallest child playing at his feet. "You should all be more like this child," he said to the listening crowd. "It is only with a child's trust and simplicity that you shall enter the kingdom of God."

*(**Matthew 19**:13–15; **Mark 10**:13–16; **Luke 18**:15–17)*

LAZARUS

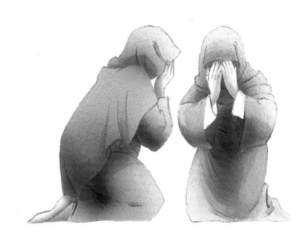

Lazarus, a friend of Jesus, was dying. His sisters, Mary and Martha, sent word to Jesus that he was ill. But when Jesus reached their home, Lazarus was already dead. Martha and Mary came to greet him. "Lord, if you had been with him when he was first ill," they sobbed, "he would have been healed." They took Jesus to the tomb where Lazarus had been laid to rest.

"Roll away the stone that covers the entrance," Jesus told them. Wondering, they did as he asked. Jesus looked up toward heaven: "Father, I know you have always heard my prayers. Now let everyone see that I do your will."

Jesus faced the tomb and cried, "Lazarus, come out!" In joy and amazement the people watched as Lazarus walked out of the tomb.

(John 11:1–43)

JESUS ENTERS JERUSALEM

Although many people now believed in Jesus and the kingdom of God, he had powerful enemies. The high priests and lawyers saw him as a threat to the ruling power of Rome. They tried to trap him with questions so that they could arrest him for stirring up rebellion. The people's love for him frightened them.

When the feast of Passover came, no one believed Jesus would go to Jerusalem. The Apostles begged him not to go. "You will surely be arrested," they cried. But they could not persuade him. Riding humbly on a donkey, Jesus entered the gates of Jerusalem.

Thousands had heard of his coming and lined the road as he passed. They spread palm leaves on the road before him and praised him as their Lord. "Blessed is he who comes in the name of God!" they cried.

(Matthew 21; Mark 11; 12:1–34; Luke 19:28–48; 20:1–39; John 7:25–44; 12:12–19)

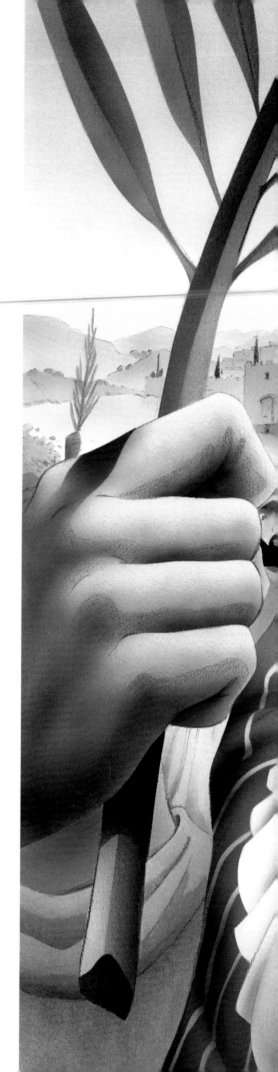

THE LAST SUPPER

Jesus knew that in Jerusalem he would be betrayed and put to death. He warned the Apostles that this would be the last Passover feast he would share with them.

That evening, Jesus and his Apostles met in the room prepared for their meal. They were horrified when he told them, "This is the last night I will eat this bread and drink this wine. Tonight I will be arrested."

Then he took some bread, broke it into pieces, and divided it among the Apostles. "This is my body," he told them. "I offer it as a sacrifice for all mankind. Eat it in memory of me."

Then he filled a glass with wine. "This is my blood," he said, passing it to each Apostle in turn. "It will be shed for you and for all men. Drink this in memory of me."

*(**Matthew 16**:21–28; **20**:17–19; **26**:17–30;*
***Mark 8**:31–38; **10**:32–34; **14**:12–26; **Luke 18**:31–34;*
***22**:7–23; **John 12**:20–36; **13**:18–21)*

THE BETRAYAL

Jesus knew one of his closest friends would betray him. Judas Iscariot had been tempted by Satan and agreed to betray Jesus in return for thirty pieces of silver.

After the Last Supper, Jesus went to pray in the Garden of Gethsemene. A band of soldiers arrived, led by Judas. "You should arrest the man I greet with a kiss," he told them. He went to Jesus and kissed him. "Have you betrayed me, Judas?" Jesus asked him sorrowfully. The other Apostles wanted to fight so that Jesus could escape, but he went with the soldiers calmly.

Alone in the garden, Judas suddenly realized the terrible thing he had done. Crying out in horror, he threw the thirty pieces of silver to the ground in disgust. He could not live with the guilt of his betrayal and hanged himself.

(*Matthew 26*:14–16; *26*:36–56; *27*:1–10; *Mark 14*:32–50; *Luke 22*:1–6; *22*:39–54; *John 18*:1–12)

JESUS BEFORE PILATE

Jesus was taken before the high council, known as the Sanhedrin. They questioned him harshly about his teachings and asked him if he were the Son of God. "Yes, it is as you say," replied Jesus.

The council accused Jesus of blasphemy and took him to the Roman governor, Pontius Pilate. Pilate also asked Jesus if he were the King of the Jews. Again Jesus replied, "Yes, it is as you say." The Sanhedrin demanded that Jesus be put to death, but Pilate could see no reason for such harshness.

At that time it was the custom for one prisoner to be released during the Passover festival. Jesus and a vicious criminal called Barabbas were the only prisoners. When Pilate asked whom he should release, the crowd called for Barabbas.

Pilate tried to reason with the council and the crowd, but they demanded Jesus' death so strongly that at last he gave in to them. Jesus was led away to be crucified.

*(**Matthew 26**:57–68; **27**:11–26; **Mark 14**:53–65; **15**:1–15; **Luke 22**:66–71; **23**:1–25; **John 18**:28–40; **19**:1–16)*

49

CARRYING THE CROSS

As the soldiers led Jesus out of the governor's palace, they mocked him cruelly. They beat him and spat at him and placed a crown of thorns upon his head.

"Hail, King of the Jews!" they laughed.

The cross was brought forward, and Jesus was made to carry it on his shoulders through the streets. The soldiers forced a man called Simon, from Cyrene, to help Jesus bear the weight.

A large crowd followed Jesus, many of them weeping for him. "Do not weep for me," Jesus told them. "You should be weeping for yourselves and for your children, for there is much suffering ahead for you."

(Matthew 27:13–32; Mark 15:21–22; Luke 23:26–31; John 19:16–17)

THE CRUCIFIXION

The place of execution was called Golgotha, or Place of the Skull. Here the soldiers nailed Jesus to the cross and crucified him. Two robbers were crucified with him at the same time.

Above Jesus' head hung a sign that said, "The King of the Jews." The priests and lawyers came to mock Jesus. "He is the Son of God," they laughed. "And he cannot even save himself!"

After Jesus had hung on the cross for many hours, a heavy darkness spread across the land. Suddenly Jesus cried out, "My God, why have you forsaken me?" The crowd waited in awe to see what would happen.

Jesus cried out once more to God, then his spirit left him, and he died. At the same moment the earth shook, and the temple curtain tore in two. The followers of Jesus took him down from the cross and laid him in a tomb.

*(**Matthew 27**:32–56; **Mark 15**:21–41; **Luke 23**:26–49; **John 19**:18–42)*

53

THE RESURRECTION

After three days had passed, Mary Magdalene, one of the disciples, visited Jesus' tomb. To her dismay the tomb was open and the body of Jesus was missing. As she began to weep at her loss, a shining angel appeared. "You should not be unhappy," it said. "You should be glad because Jesus has risen from the dead."

Then a voice called to her, and a man stood before her. At first she did not recognize him. Then to her great amazement and joy, her eyes were opened, and she saw that it was Jesus.

Full of awe and wonder, she hurried into town to tell the other disciples. Although Jesus had told them that the Son of God must die and rise again, they had not truly believed it.

(Matthew 28:1–10; Mark 16:1–11; Luke 24:1–12; John 20:1–18)

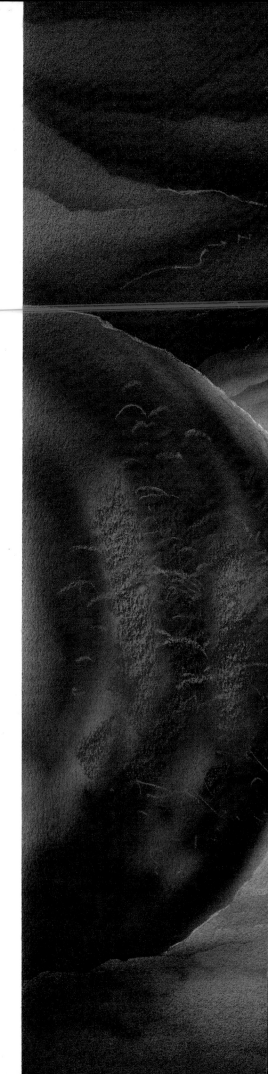

THE REVELATION

Later that same day, Jesus appeared to two of his disciples as they traveled to Emmaus. They did not recognize him, but welcomed him as a traveling companion. "We were just speaking about Jesus of Nazareth," they told him. "We hoped that he would be the savior of the Jews, but the council arrested and crucified him. Some have claimed to have seen him risen from the tomb, but this cannot be true."

Jesus rebuked them for their lack of faith. "Was it not foretold that the Son of God must die, then rise again?" he asked them. In wonder they recognized him, but he disappeared before them.

That evening Jesus appeared to the Apostles. Even they did not believe he had risen from the dead and were afraid, thinking he was a ghost. "Touch me," he told them. "See the wounds in my hands and feet. I am no ghost."

(Mark 16:12–14; Luke 24:13–48; John 19:30)

THE ASCENSION

The Apostles went out to the Mount of Olives, where they had once prayed with Jesus. There he appeared to them for the last time. "You must prepare," he told them. "The Holy Spirit will soon come upon you. On that day you must go out and spread the Word of God to all nations. You must teach mankind all that you have seen and learned while I was with you."

Jesus then blessed the Apostles, who bowed their heads in worship. He rose into the sky, went into a cloud, and ascended into heaven, to sit at God's right hand.

And just as Jesus had said, the Holy Spirit came upon the Apostles and gave them the strength and wisdom to go out and preach the Word of God.

Wherever they traveled many listened, many believed, and many were saved, just as Jesus had foretold.

*(**Matthew 28**:16–20; **Mark 16**:15–20; **Luke 24**:44–53; **John 20**:21)*

59